BUSHMEN
A CHANGING WAY OF LIFE

BUSHMEN

A CHANGING WAY OF LIFE

Photographs by ANTHONY BANNISTER
Text by DAVID LEWIS-WILLIAMS

STRUIK

Struik Publishers
(a member of The Struik Group (Pty) Ltd)
Struik House
Oswald Pirow Street
Foreshore
Cape Town
8001

Reg. No.: 63/00203/07

First published 1991

Designer: Joan Sutton
Typesetting by BellSet, Cape Town
Reproduction by Unifoto (Pty) Ltd, Cape Town
Printed and Bound by Kyodo Printing Co (Pte) Ltd, Singapore

ISBN 1 86825 178 0

FRONTISPIECE *The wise humour of the Bushmen shows clearly in their wrinkled features.*

PREVIOUS PAGES *The Kalahari of Botswana and Namibia, where most of the surviving Bushmen live, is not a uniformly barren desert; much of it is an extensive, flat grassland with numerous trees.*

OPPOSITE *With his bow and hunting bag, a hunter looks out over the vastness of the Kalahari at dawn; he will know where the best hunting is likely to be found.*

INTRODUCTION

ABOVE *In the depths of the Kalahari, radios and tape recorders are a link with the world beyond.*

TOP *Today Western clothing is worn in combination with the more traditional garments and beads.*

The very word 'Bushmen' conjures up images of a people living a happy, carefree existence in harmony with nature and far from the stresses of cities and civilization. These images are so vivid that museums sometimes associate their Bushman, or, to use a more academic word, San, exhibit with natural rather than cultural history – with the animals of Africa rather than with its people.

There is, of course, truth in the belief that the Bushmen's way of life harmonized with nature far better than that of many other people, certainly better than modern Western industrialism. But, in the last analysis, they have become enshrouded in what could be called the 'Great Bushman Myth', a set of changing perceptions that has done them somewhat more harm than good.

The modern Myth is quite different from the original version. In recent times, the Bushmen, and their supposed Shangri-la in the depths of the Kalahari Desert, have been seen as an image of Western romantic ideals rather than as real people struggling with real problems. Their supposed remoteness, both geographical and spiritual, has been much exploited by Western writers who extol their wisdom and gentleness. They are presented as a people whom history has passed by, a people preserving the lost innocence of humankind, childlike yet profound, simple, yet subtly attuned to the animals around them and to the changing face of the desert. In short, a people from whom arrogant Westerners can learn humility and draw spiritual sustenance.

The first Europeans to meet the Bushmen did not share these environmentalist and mystical views about them. True, they saw them as akin to the creatures of nature, but at that time attitudes towards animals were very different from the modern environmentalists' ideas. To the early settlers, the Bushmen were merely wild, dangerous animals, fit only to be driven out by the advance of superior peoples. As *Bosjesmans*, the name the Dutch colonists gave them, suggests, they were believed to lurk among the bushes, waiting to spring out on unwary travellers. Some people believed, quite incorrectly, that the Bushmen were herders who, having lost their cattle, had become footloose bandits preying on innocent people. Even today, some people use 'Bushman' as an insult. The settlers were baffled by their lack of chiefs and their puzzling religion, and, worse, disgusted by their appearance and their nomadic lifestyle. Forgetting that it was the Bushmen's land in the first place, the colonists inveighed against their reluctance to work as labourers on white-owned farms.

At the beginning of the 20th century, the celebrated colonial historian George McCall Theal summed up these ideas when he wrote that the Bushmen 'were of no benefit to any other section of the human family, they were incapable of improvement, and as it was impossible for civilized men to live on the same soil with them, it was for the world's good that they should make room for a higher race'.

When the settlers first encountered them, the Bushmen lived in an area covering most of southern Africa, and not just in desert regions as they do today. Many had been in contact with black farmers for centuries, but they nevertheless still preserved aspects of their ancient way of life, including some remarkable skills which have led to the Bushmen achieving worldwide fame.

Possibly the most vaunted of their skills are those employed in hunting, using bow and poisoned arrows. Their now-famous poison was obtained from a variety of sources – including snake venom, plant saps and the grub of a beetle – and was remarkably potent. Even a small scratch from an arrow could lead to death, as there was no antidote for some of the poisons.

The construction of the arrows was as ingenious as the poisons. Each arrow comprised a reed shaft, a torpedo-shaped link made from bone or wood, a short reed collar and, finally, the envenomed point – originally made of bone but, in more recent times, of iron obtained from either black or white farmers. When such an arrow struck its target, the impact drove the link into the collar, splitting it, and thus allowing the shaft to fall away while the poisoned point remained firmly embedded in the animal. The poison did not, however, take immediate effect; frequently hunters had to track a large wounded animal, a giraffe or an eland, for many days before they found its carcass. Sometimes the hyenas reached their prey before they did.

The need to find a wounded animal as soon as possible, and the comparatively short range of their small bows, made good tracking and stalking essential. It was not for nothing that almost supernatural tracking skills became part of the Bushman Myth. A good tracker could find the spoor of a wounded animal amongst the confused marks of a herd and follow it for days, never losing it, and always able to gauge how much longer it would be able to keep going.

The women were no less skilful in their tasks. They could detect the smallest wisp of a dried up stalk and know at once that it signalled the presence of a succulent, edible root or tuber deep underground. In times of severe drought, these plant resources provided a valuable – in the driest parts of the Kalahari, indispensible – source of water.

A woman kept the plant foods she collected for her own family, but meat, a less easily acquired foodstuff, was always shared among the people of the camp – even with casual visitors. When a wounded animal had been tracked down and killed, it was cut up, and the meat was taken back to the camp. The returning party, especially the successful hunter, was received with great acclaim, but the animal actually belonged to the person who owned the arrow that had killed it. This person was not necessarily the hunter who had shot the animal, as people often exchanged arrows. The owner of the arrow then distributed the meat so that everyone received a fair portion. In this way, the chancy outcome of hunting was neutralized: a long run of bad luck did not mean that a man and his family would starve. Sharing was at the heart of the Bushman way of life; it was the cornerstone of their morality.

The Bushmen's dependence on hunting and plants for food meant that they had to keep moving, not aimlessly wandering across the landscape as the Myth has it, but following an annual round that took them to seasonally

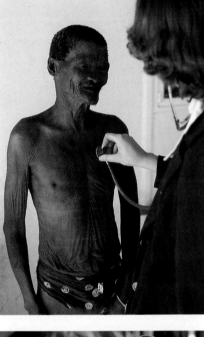

ABOVE T'

ABOVE *Modern transport has replaced travel on foot.*

ABOVE RIGHT *The traditional Bushman systems of barter and gift giving are gradually being superseded by Western commerce; arrows are now bought with money.*

ripening foods and sources of water. Nothing could be left to chance. Far from not using, and having no rights to, the land, their whole life was geared to its careful exploitation. At some times of the year, camps would break up into smaller family units to permit better use of meagre resources; they then reunited at a predetermined time and place. Constant splitting up and reuniting helped to maintain links, often by marriage, with camps in distant regions. Then, if the rains failed in their own region, they could join people in better watered areas.

Partly because of this fission and fusion of camps, the Bushmen did not have chiefs in the same sense that settled, agricultural people do. Bushmen could not therefore respond to the age-old explorer's command, 'Take me to your leader!'. Although some people inevitably had more influence than others, all decisions were talked about by everyone, men and women, until agreement was achieved. Today we see this sort of political arrangement as enviable, but the early white travellers found it merely indicative of a low level of civilization.

Even more perplexing to the Europeans was the Bushmen's religion. Some exasperated missionaries declared that they had no religion at all, or that they themselves did not know what they believed. The missionaries were mistaken: the Bushmen had a very subtle religion with a rich store of highly complex and symbolic folktales. The now-extinct /Xam Bushmen who lived in the Cape Colony south of the Orange River believed in a being called /Kaggen, a name sometimes translated as 'Mantis'. This translation led to the false belief that the Bushmen worshipped an insect. In fact, the insect was only one of /Kaggen's manifestations. He could also turn into an eland, an eagle, a hartebeest, a hare and a snake. He was in fact a protean being whose influence could be felt across all of life. As one 19th-century Bushman put it, '/Kaggen can be by you, without you seeing him.'

Another man from the same time said that /Kaggen reminded him of the Guy Fawkes masks he had seen the settlers' children wearing: ' They change their faces, for they want us … to think that it is not a person. /Kaggen also cheats people so that we may not know it is he.' After all, people in all times and places have felt incapable of pinning down and defining divinity. When Bushmen wanted to express the elusive, multi-faceted nature of divinity, they turned, understandably enough, to the diversity of the animal life around them.

The Kalahari !Kung Bushmen to the north expressed the complexity of divinity in another way. They believed in two gods, a greater god who lived in the east and a lesser who lived in the west. Neither god was completely good or bad. Associated with these gods were the spirits of the dead, somewhat vague beings who did not represent specific ancestors and who cannot be said to indicate the practice of ancestor worship. These spirits were believed to shoot mystical 'arrows of sickness' into people, small invisible darts that caused disease and death.

To protect themselves from the 'arrows of sickness' and other perils, the Bushmen had shamans, or medicine people. In recent times, about half of the men living in the Kalahari, and a third of the women, were shamans. These people were not an elite priesthood – they hunted and collected plant foods with everyone else – but they had a special ability to enter a state of trance, either at a large dance or in more solitary circumstances. In trance, they cured the sick by laying their trembling hands on them and drawing out the 'arrows of sickness' or whatever else was harming them. They were also believed to go on out-of-body journeys, to make rain and to guide antelope into the hunters' ambush.

At a large shamanic dance, the women clapped the rhythm and sang ancient power songs, while the men danced around them and eventually entered trance – for them, the spirit world. The clapping, singing and dancing was believed to activate a supernatural potency that resided in the songs and in the shamans themselves. The American anthropologist Lorna Marshall who, together with her family, worked with !Kung Bushmen in the early 1950s, likened this potency to electricity: it is a power that can be harnessed for the good of humankind, but intense concentrations, if allowed to get out of control, can kill people.

Supernatural power – and the dance that activates it – lies behind the rock paintings and engravings for which the Bushmen are justly famous. The groups who made the art no longer exist. The people presently living in the Kalahari do not recall a tradition of painting or engraving on rocks. When asked about the paintings in the Tsodilo Hills in northwestern Botswana, some simply say that God put them there; the paintings are God's animals. This sort of remark has been taken to mean that these Bushmen do not know anything at all about the art, but that may not be entirely correct.

Using the power of the great animals, especially /Kaggen's favourite creature, the eland, shamans entered the spirit world and, in so doing, assumed the form of an animal. This animal was probably the one whose supernatural potency they believed they were able to activate when they journeyed to the spirit world; the potency was named after the animal, but was also inside them. When they reached the spirit world, they saw all God's creatures, terrifying spirits, and even God himself. When they returned to the 'real' world, they told people about their experiences, each

ABOVE *As the traditional way of life becomes increasingly less viable, the Bushmen have taken to more Western life styles. The hunter-gatherer has become a tradesman.*

TOP *Even the remotest Bushmen are familiar with Coca-Cola, and have been for some decades.*

9

ABOVE *These days, the Bushmen recognize the necessity of Western education, and encourage their children to attend school.*

TOP *New art forms are being developed to supply a growing tourist industry.*

account being received as a true revelation, even though it may have contradicted another shaman's experience; the Bushmen were as open to different opinions in religion as they were in politics. Then, shamans who were also painters took the powerful blood of an eland and mixed it with various pigments, some of which were likewise believed to have potency, and, in a now tranquil state, carefully painted their visions and their power animals on the rock face.

Each image was more than just a picture of something else – an animal or a vision. Each was a thing in itself, with its own power and life. As the trancing shamans danced in the rock shelters where they lived, these painted visions triggered, and then mixed with, their own visions of spiritual realms. As the centuries went by, paintings of these visions piled up, one on top of the other, in, for Westerners, confusing palimpsests but, for the Bushmen themselves, unfathomable reservoirs of power.

Changes in this traditional way of life first began to come about approximately 2 000 years ago, when the Bushmen first encountered black farmers with cattle and sheep. Since that first contact, there has been constant interchange between the Bushmen and their black neighbours that, as archaeological evidence shows, extended deep into the Kalahari. Some groups of Bushmen adopted sheep-keeping as a way of life, and called themselves Khoikhoi, Men of Men; much later the colonists called them Hottentots. It seems that others became farmers for a while and then reverted to hunting and gathering. Certainly, some became professional rain-makers and ritual specialists for black farmers in the south, where much intermarriage took place. This mixing allowed the distinctive clicks of the various Bushman languages to become part of Xhosa and Zulu. All this evidence shows that it is simply another part of the Bushman Myth that they were unchanging Stone Age fossils, living isolated lives in the lost world of the Kalahari until some venturesome whites 'discovered' them.

The interaction between Bushmen and black farmers and Khoikhoi herders continued until a new threat appeared – the arrival of the Europeans. Just over 300 years ago, Dutch settlers established a provisioning post at the Cape of Good Hope, but, even before that time, passing ships had started bartering with the Khoikhoi – beads and trinkets for cattle and sheep. This hitherto unknown commercialization of stock started a chain reaction that reached far into the interior, and disrupted the traditional ways of life. The Dutch settlement expanded rapidly from the Cape, penetrating deep into the Bushmen's land. The colonists' rifles shot out the game, and their cattle overgrazed the veld. There was no possibility of the sort of rapprochement that developed between the Bushmen and the black farmers. On the contrary, it was literally a fight to the death.

The horrendous misconceptions held by the early colonists as to the nature of the Bushmen led them to mount terrible punitive raids against these people, killing the adults and taking the children into slavery, until the southern groups were virtually wiped out. Those who escaped the commandos intermarried with both white and black farmers or were forced to accept a life of serfdom.

The only place where traditional ways survived was the inhospitable Kalahari Desert. There, groups continued to maintain their values, living on the fringes of the more powerful black ranchers, and, later, the white farmers. Until recently, some worked for farmers, periodically returning to the desert to join their people.

That was the Kalahari of the 1950s, when the first large-scale anthropological studies of the Bushmen were undertaken – not of a lost people, but of the remnants of a people with a long, varied history. The anthropologists were, however, in some ways like the travellers and missionaries of earlier centuries: although they would have been horrified by the idea, they were the forerunners, though not the cause, of total destruction, harbingers of commerce, migrant labour and a sedentary life style, as, soon after their work with the Bushmen began, farmers and traders moved into the area.

For centuries, the Kalahari Bushmen had lived on the fringes of other communities. During this time, their richer neighbours saw to it that they remained in comparative poverty by denying them rights to the land. Before long, in both Botswana and Namibia, they found their territory drastically reduced. In Namibia the position was exacerbated by the South African administration's policy of racial 'homelands', and the Bushmen's territory continued to shrink. One man told Megan Biesele, an anthropologist who has worked with them for many years, 'Long ago when we went to our new camps, we brought embers from our old camps. When has this government ever come to us with an ember?'.

Instead, poverty and eviction has been their lot: 'I'm not a person who knows the names of years, but I know that back when the Germans were fighting their war, we had already been here since our father's fathers … Even Windhoek was long ago Bushmanland, and Okakarara and Etosha Pan – these were all Bushmanland'.

Behind all the poverty and suffering that the Bushmen were forced to endure lay the belief that these nomadic people of the desert were congenitally unsuited to a farming life; because they had no powerful chiefs, they were thought, quite incorrectly, to be incapable of looking after themselves.

Faced with the Bushmen's worsening poverty and starvation, some of the anthropologists who studied them in the 1950s came to their aid. The Marshall family established the Ju/wa Bushman Development Foundation and assisted them in forming a farmers' cooperative that can negotiate with the newly independent Namibian government. This may well be their last hope of survival as a people.

Despite the Bushmen's worldwide fame, the myths that have gathered around them have misrepresented them. The media still portray them as childlike innocents marvelling at Coca-Cola bottles and living in an Eden untouched by the modern world. Harassed city-dwellers see them as Nature's own ecologists, living within a spiritual environment. The Bushmen have become a figment of Western civilization's sentimental dreams of primitive innocence.

A couple of centuries ago, the Myth portrayed them as subhuman, dirty, treacherous and ignorant. The modern Myth goes in the other direction and does them equal disservice. Eden, if it ever existed, has gone; poverty and a need to struggle for their rights have swiftly taken its place.

ABOVE *Although the Kalahari Bushmen have no tradition of painting or knowledge of rock art, they have learnt to produce striking murals.*

TOP *The advance of Western culture has even brought about a change in the playthings of Bushman children.*

11

ABOVE *A Bushman woman cuts strips of animal hide, which will be used for binding bundles, amongst other things.*

LEFT *A woman prepares traditional clothing as she cares for her child: Bushmen devote a great deal of time to their children.*

ABOVE *Pendants made from plastic or glass beads are a popular style of adornment.*

ABOVE LEFT *A young woman wears beads together with a modern, printed head scarf.*

RIGHT *Trade beads are taking the place of traditional beads, which were made from pieces of ostrich eggshell carefully filed to approximately the same size and shape with a stone.*

RIGHT *A woman waits patiently while her friend adorns her hair with pieces of beadwork.*

FAR RIGHT *In all her finery, a woman rests while out gathering plant foods for the evening meal.*

BELOW *A woman applies a traditional mark, said to represent the gemsbok, to her child's forehead.*

ABOVE *As evening approaches at this traditional Bushman camp in the Kalahari, the people prepare to relax around the fire.*

ABOVE *The traditional grass huts of the Bushmen provide shelter from the burning desert sun.*

LEFT *It is the task of the women to collect the bundles of long grass which are needed to build their dwellings. The men build a frame of tapered saplings: they are planted in a rough circle and tied together at the top. The women then thatch the frame with the bundles of grass.*

ABOVE LEFT *Bushmen store many things, especially ostrich eggshells filled with water, under the sand. These will be unearthed later, when needed.*

LEFT *A medicine man treats a patient with the traditional antelope horn, which he uses to suck the sickness out of the man.*

RIGHT *A large tortoise is a lucky find, as it is a source of food and the shell can later be used as a container. In a life where much is hard to come by, little is allowed to go to waste.*

ABOVE *As the sun sets, a family gathers round the fire for the evening meal of roots, berries and, if they are lucky, meat.*

LEFT *Smoking is a favourite pastime for both men and women.*

ABOVE *In the cold Kalahari nights, the temperature often falls below freezing point, and a fire is a welcome source of warmth.*

ABOVE RIGHT *The fire is the focus of social contact; it is here that the events of the day, as well as traditional folktales, are recounted.*

RIGHT *Traditionally, a fire was made by twirling a stick against another piece of wood, which was held in place by the foot. The heat caused by the resultant friction would then ignite the dry tinder placed around the point of contact.*

ABOVE *The thumb piano, an instrument found in many parts of Africa, is also a popular source of music for the Bushmen.*

LEFT *One traditional Bushman instrument is played by plucking strings made from sinew. Curved sticks are used to adjust the tension of the stings, and a hollow wooden base acts as a resonator.*

LEFT *A woman lovingly and pensively cradles her child. In the close-knit community of the Bushmen, the young are treasured and looked after by all, being constantly passed from the care of one adult to that of another.*

RIGHT *A thoughtful young woman and her baby stave off the evening cold with an old blanket.*

BELOW *Children are allowed a lot of freedom to play as their fancy takes them.*

ABOVE *After the summer rains, the usually dry pans of the Kalahari fill with water, providing a favourite playground for children.*

ABOVE RIGHT *Small children, decorated with beads, play with beetles in the sand.*

ABOVE RIGHT *Two young boys make pets out of some ostrich chicks that they have found.*

RIGHT *The hold that a tortoise like this has on life is a fairly tenuous one; animals are valued more as a food source than as pets.*

FAR RIGHT *Children play with a feather attached to a weighted string. They throw it into the air, and then try to catch it on the end of a stick.*

ABOVE *Two!Kung Bushman children play happily together.*

ABOVE LEFT *This toy is made from a piece of wood attached to some sinew. The sinew is twisted and then pulled, causing the piece of wood to spin round and round, making a roaring noise.*

LEFT *A popular traditional game involves young boys linking their legs together; the one who retains his balance the longest is the winner.*

LEFT *Naturally, many of the games children play are imitations of the things adults do, and this also serves as a learning experience. Here, a young boy takes aim with a bow and arrow.*

RIGHT *A hunter carefully carves a new bow stave. The Bushman bow is small, and does not have a great range, so the Bushmen rely on their considerable skill as hunters to get within shooting range of their prey.*

ABOVE *A number of men work together to prepare poison arrows. The arrows are constructed so that the shaft falls off on impact, allowing the head to remain imbedded in the flesh of the animal that has been shot.*

ABOVE *The string of a Bushman bow is prepared from the sinews that run down the length of a large antelope's back.*

TOP *The poison used in hunting is squeezed out of the larvae of a beetle, and the iron arrow point is bound with grass to allow the poison to adhere. The poison is put well behind the piercing surface of the head, as a precaution against poisoning the hunters as they handle the arrows.*

ABOVE *A weary Bushman hunter takes a break to refresh himself at a pan.*

TOP *The quivers in which Bushman hunters carry their arrows are made from the bark of a tree. The kokerboom (quiver tree) is so named because it is one of the trees favoured by the Bushmen for this purpose.*

ABOVE LEFT *Bushmen are able to run at a steady pace for great distances as they track animals or pursue a wounded antelope.*

ABOVE *Two men examine the spoor of a large antelope to determine the animal's condition and to estimate how far it will run before the poison of their arrows finally kills it.*

LEFT *The tracking skills of the Bushmen are legendary. Here, two hunters follow the tracks of an antelope through the long grass of the Kalahari.*

ABOVE *An elephant is a rarely encountered but valuable find, as its meat will provide food for a large number of people for many days.*

ABOVE LEFT *Hunters do not speak to each other for fear of frightening the animals away, and all communication is done by means of hand signals. Here a man signals that he has sighted a giraffe spoor.*

Stalking is a crucial part of the hunt: it is important that the hunters get as close as they can to their prospective prey, as their bows are small and do not have a great range.

LEFT *Staying as still as possible, a hunter takes careful aim. Even after the animal has been shot, the hunt is far from over, as the arrows are far too light to kill, and the animal will take flight, running until the slow-acting poison takes effect.*

BELOW *Success! The wounded animal - in this case a kudu - has finally been tracked down and dispatched with a spear.*

Once the animal has been killed, if it is too large to carry home in one piece, it is butchered on site - a task that may take many hours. After the meat has been cut into manageable pieces, it is hung on sticks and carried back to camp, where the women and children joyfully welcome the successful hunters. Any meat that is not eaten immediately is cut into strips and hung out to dry.

ABOVE AND RIGHT *Although a Bushman will not set out specifically to hunt a porcupine or python, it is no trouble to bring one home for the pot if the burrows of these animals are seen, as they provide much good meat.*

OVERLEAF *The distribution of the meat is the prerogative of the owner of the arrow that killed the animal, and everyone receives a fair portion.*

ABOVE AND LEFT *The Bushmen who live in the Okavango swamps in northern Botswana have become expert fishermen, traversing the many rivers of the region in dugout canoes. Much of the catch is laid out in the sun to dry, so that it can be stored for a long time.*

ABOVE *Bushmen are highly skilled at setting snares for small antelope. A piece of cord is tied in a noose, which is pegged into the ground, and concealed under sand and leaves. The other end of the cord is attached to a sapling anchored firmly to the ground, so that there is tension between the noose and the sapling. Once an animal steps on the noose, the trigger mechanism in its centre is released, the sapling whips back, and the noose tightens around the animal's leg.*

RIGHT *Ostrich eggs, a favoured food source among the Bushmen, are tied up in bundles of grass before they are carried home.*

Ostrich-egg omelette is a favourite dish among the Bushmen. A hole is pierced in the shell, and the contents are stirred. A fire is made in a hollow and allowed to burn to ashes. The contents of the egg are then poured onto the ashes of the fire and cooked. The empty shell is used as a water container, or to make beads for decoration.

ABOVE *Meat is a much valued commodity among the Bushmen, but not always available, and the daily collection of roots, berries and fruits provides an important part of what is essentially a vegetarian diet.*

RIGHT *A woman carries her child in a sling while she gathers berries for her family.*

ABOVE *The large bags which the women take with them when they search for edible foodstuffs are made from animal skins.*

LEFT *Bushman women are very skilled at discerning the mere wisp of a plant which indicates that an edible root is deep underground.*

RIGHT *A man scoops the inside of an edible root into his mouth.*

ABOVE *Honey is a greatly desired food among the Bushmen, and a curious relationship with a bird known as the honey guide allows them to find it. When a honey guide is sighted, the Bushmen follow it until the bird, calling harshly, leads them to a hive. The bees are then smoked out, and the Bushmen take the honey, while the bird claims the wax and the larvae.*

RIGHT *Rough ladders and pegs driven into a baobab tree allow a man to climb up to a hive.*

FAR RIGHT *A group of Bushmen take honey from a baobab tree.*

ABOVE AND RIGHT *Ostrich eggshells are often used as water containers; after they have been filled, they are plugged with a grass stopper and buried underground.*

LEFT *Water is extremely scarce for much of the year in the Kalahari, and Bushmen will often dig large holes to uncover a water source. In spite of this scarcity of water, Bushmen do not mind others drinking from their water holes, as long as common courtesy is shown by the person wishing to drink.*

RIGHT *Using a reed, a man sucks water out of a hollow in the fork of a baobab tree.*

LEFT AND BELOW *One of the most dependable sources of water in the Kalahari is the moisture-filled melons and tubers that grow there. These are cut open, and the insides are squeezed to obtain the precious liquid.*

Children the world over love to play in water, but in the Kalahari this pleasure is restricted to times of heavy rain - usually between January and March – when the pans fill with water to create large, shallow pools.

ABOVE *The healing or trance dance is the Bushmen's most important religious ritual. As the women clap the rhythm and sing power songs, the men dance in a circle around them. During the dance, medicine men lay their hands on everyone present - even visiting anthropologists - to draw out the 'arrows of sickness'.*

FAR LEFT AND LEFT *Cocoons are dried out and filled with small stones to make dancing rattles. These are tied onto the legs of the medicine men before they perform their dance.*

RIGHT *In a frenzy of trance, a medicine man thrusts his head into the fire. The trance into which they go, the Bushmen believe, is their entry into the spirit world.*

ABOVE *These rock paintings in the Tsodilo Hills of northwestern Botswana show animals regarded as a source of supernatural power, as well as hand prints.*

ABOVE RIGHT *At Twyfelfontein, Namibia, hundreds of animals and their spoor have been chipped into the rocks.*

OVERLEAF *These paintings in the Natal Drakensberg show eland, and large, cloaked medicine men, who, in their trance experience, have hoofs instead of feet.*

*At one time, Bushman peoples occupied most of southern Africa.
Constant encroachment on their land, however, has left them
confined to the Kalahari regions of Botswana and Namibia. In the
rest of the subcontinent, only their engravings and paintings remain
as a reminder that they once lived there.*